SUZANNE BYRD

Fractured, Yet Whole

*A Woman's Journey Through Borderline Personality
Disorder*

First edition

This book was professionally typeset on Reedsy.
Find out more at reedsy.com

Contents

1

Understanding Borderline Personality Disorder

When you hear the term "borderline," what comes to mind? For many, it's a word drenched in misunderstanding—on the "borderline" of what, exactly? For decades, the name itself has been debated among mental health professionals, but what remains constant is the reality of the condition: Borderline Personality Disorder (BPD) is a complex mental health challenge, often misunderstood and deeply stigmatized. For women, the experience of living with BPD can be uniquely shaped by societal expectations, gender roles, and the challenges of navigating mental health systems that often fail to meet their needs.

In this chapter, we will explore the foundations of BPD: what it is, how it manifests, and why it disproportionately affects women. Along the way, we will meet Emma, a 28-year-old woman whose early struggles with BPD highlight the challenges of diagnosis and understanding.

What is Borderline Personality Disorder?

Borderline Personality Disorder is a mental health condition characterized by pervasive instability in emotions, self-image, relationships, and behavior. It is often described as living with a raw emotional nerve, where even the smallest touch can cause excruciating pain. People with BPD frequently experience intense mood swings, fear of abandonment, impulsive actions, and a chronic sense of emptiness. These symptoms can make daily life feel chaotic and relationships tumultuous.

The Diagnostic and Statistical Manual of Mental Disorders (DSM-5) outlines nine key criteria for diagnosing BPD. To meet the diagnosis, an individual must exhibit at least five of these symptoms, which include:

Frantic efforts to avoid real or imagined abandonment.

A pattern of unstable and intense interpersonal relationships.

Unstable self-image or sense of self.

Impulsive behaviors in at least two areas (e.g., spending, substance use, reckless driving).

Recurrent suicidal behavior, gestures, or self-harming actions.

Emotional instability due to a marked reactivity of mood.

Chronic feelings of emptiness.

Intense or inappropriate anger.

Transient, stress-related paranoia or dissociative symptoms.

While these criteria provide a clinical framework, they fail to capture the lived experience of BPD—its nuances, its intensity, and its impact on the individual and their loved ones.

The Gendered Face of BPD

Research suggests that around 75% of individuals diagnosed with BPD are women. This statistic has led to debates about whether the condition is truly more prevalent in women or whether diagnostic biases play a role. Women are often socialized to prioritize relationships and emotional expression, which may make BPD symptoms like fear of abandonment and emotional dysregulation more noticeable to clinicians. Additionally, women are more likely to seek help for mental health issues, potentially skewing diagnostic rates.

For Emma, societal expectations compounded her struggles. Raised in a family where vulnerability was seen as weakness, she learned early on to suppress her emotions. By her teenage years, this suppression erupted into outbursts of anger and despair, leaving her feeling isolated and misunderstood. When she first sought help, her symptoms were dismissed as "teenage angst" and "attention-seeking," a common experience for women with BPD.

The Emotional Landscape of BPD

At the heart of BPD is emotional dysregulation. Imagine experiencing every emotion at full volume, with no way to turn it down. For people with BPD, this intensity can be both overwhelming and isolating. They may go from euphoric joy to debilitating despair within hours, often in response to seemingly minor triggers.

Emma described her emotions as "a storm I couldn't escape." A simple disagreement with her boyfriend could spiral into catastrophic thoughts: He's going to leave me. I'll be alone forever. What's the point of trying anymore? These emotional reactions weren't just "dramatic" or "overreacting"—they were the result of a hypersensitive emotional system, likely shaped by a combination of genetics and early life experiences.

Childhood Roots and Trauma

While not all individuals with BPD have a history of trauma, studies show a significant correlation between BPD and adverse childhood experiences, such as neglect, abuse, or unstable caregiving environments. Early experiences of invalidation— where a child's emotions are ignored or minimized—can teach them that their feelings are not trustworthy or important. This can lead to the intense fear of abandonment and difficulties with self-identity seen in BPD.

Emma's childhood was marked by inconsistency. Her mother, struggling with her own mental health issues, would vacillate between affection and cold detachment. Emma often felt like she was "walking on eggshells," never knowing when the next emotional explosion would occur. This unpredictability shaped her deep-seated fear of abandonment and her tendency to cling to relationships, even when they were unhealthy.

The Misunderstanding of BPD

BPD has long been a misunderstood diagnosis. For decades, it was viewed as untreatable, with individuals often labeled as "manipulative" or "difficult" by healthcare providers. These misconceptions have contributed to a lack of resources and support for people with BPD, leaving many to navigate their struggles alone.

Emma's experience with the healthcare system reflected these biases. After a particularly intense episode of self-harm at age 21, she was hospitalized and referred to a psychiatrist. Instead of compassion, she was met with skepticism. "You're doing this for attention," the psychiatrist said dismissively. Emma left the appointment feeling ashamed and defeated, questioning whether her pain was valid.

The Complexity of Diagnosis

Diagnosing BPD is challenging, especially because its symptoms often overlap with other conditions, such as depression, anxiety, and bipolar disorder. For women, this complexity is compounded by societal stereotypes that pathologize emotional expression. As a result, many women with BPD go undiagnosed or misdiagnosed for years, delaying access to effective treatment.

Emma was initially diagnosed with depression and anxiety, conditions she undoubtedly experienced but which didn't fully explain her intense emotional reactions, relationship struggles, and sense of emptiness. It wasn't until she connected with a therapist trained in personality disorders that she received an accurate diagnosis.

Why Diagnosis Matters

For individuals with BPD, receiving a diagnosis can be both a relief and a source of fear. On one hand, it provides a framework for understanding their struggles. On the other hand, it comes with the weight of stigma. However, a diagnosis is also the first step toward healing. With the right support, individuals with BPD can learn to manage their symptoms and build fulfilling lives.

For Emma, the diagnosis marked the beginning of a transformative journey. Through therapy, she began to understand her patterns and develop tools to navigate her emotions and relationships. While the road was not easy, it was the first time she felt truly seen and validated.

A Message of Hope

Borderline Personality Disorder is not a life sentence. While the condition can be challenging, it is also highly treatable with evidence-based therapies like Dialectical Behavior Therapy (DBT). For women like Emma, who have spent years feeling misunderstood and overwhelmed, there is hope. Understanding BPD is the first step toward breaking the cycle of stigma and empowering women to reclaim their lives.

In the chapters to come, we will dive deeper into the lived experience of BPD, exploring its impact on relationships, identity, and self-worth. We will also highlight the resilience and strength of women who, like Emma, are navigating this complex condition with courage and determination.

2

The Emotional Rollercoaster

Living with Borderline Personality Disorder (BPD) is like being on a rollercoaster you didn't choose to ride. The highs are dizzying, the lows are crushing, and there's rarely a moment of stillness. For women with BPD, this emotional intensity is both a defining characteristic and one of the most misunderstood aspects of the condition. Society often labels women as "too emotional" or "overly dramatic," making it even harder for those with BPD to seek understanding and help.

This chapter explores the inner workings of emotional dysregulation, the impact it has on daily life, and how women can begin to navigate this whirlwind. Along the way, we'll hear from Sarah, a 35-year-old woman whose emotional rollercoaster led her to both moments of despair and profound self-discovery.

The Anatomy of Emotional Dysregulation

Imagine your emotions as a volume dial. For most people, the dial can be adjusted depending on the situation—turned down during a tense meeting, turned up during a joyful celebration. For someone with BPD, that dial is broken. Emotions hit at full blast, often out of proportion to the triggering event, and linger longer than they would for others.

This heightened emotional sensitivity is partly rooted in biology. Studies suggest that individuals with BPD have hyperactive amygdalas, the part of the brain responsible for processing emotions, coupled with underactive prefrontal cortexes, which help regulate those emotions. The result is a system that feels everything intensely but struggles to manage those feelings.

For Sarah, this meant living in a state of constant reactivity. A minor disagreement with her sister could spiral into hours of crying, self-doubt, and overwhelming shame. "It felt like my emotions owned me," she recalled. "I couldn't see past the moment, no matter how hard I tried."

Triggers: The Spark to the Flame

Emotional dysregulation doesn't occur in a vacuum. For women with BPD, certain triggers—situations or interactions that evoke strong emotional reactions—can set off a cascade of feelings. These triggers are often tied to deep-seated fears, particularly the fear of abandonment or rejection.

Sarah's primary trigger was feeling ignored. At work, if her boss failed to acknowledge her contributions in a meeting, she would spend the rest of the day convinced she was going to be fired. At home, a delayed text from her boyfriend could send her into a panic, replaying worst-case scenarios in her mind. "It wasn't just that I felt hurt," she explained. "It was like I became the hurt. It consumed me."

The Cost of Intensity

Living on this emotional rollercoaster comes with a cost. For many women with BPD, the unpredictability of their emotions can strain relationships, disrupt careers, and erode self-esteem. Sarah often described herself as "too much" and feared that her intensity would drive people away.

This fear wasn't unfounded. Friends and family, unsure of how to respond to her outbursts or mood swings, would sometimes pull away. At work, her colleagues labeled her as "difficult," not understanding that her emotional reactions were beyond her control. Each instance of rejection reinforced her belief that she was unworthy of love and stability, creating a vicious cycle.

Moments of Light: The Upsides of Emotional Intensity

While the emotional rollercoaster of BPD is often overwhelming, it's not without its moments of light. Women with BPD frequently describe feeling a deep capacity for empathy, passion, and connection. When emotions are positive, they can be just as intense as the negative ones, leading to moments of profound joy and creativity.

For Sarah, these moments came in her artwork. A painter by hobby, she found that her emotional intensity allowed her to connect deeply with her subjects, capturing feelings on canvas in a way that resonated with others. "When I'm painting, it's like I can take all the chaos inside me and turn it into something beautiful," she said.

Recognizing and nurturing these strengths can be a vital part of the healing process, helping women with BPD see their emotions not just as a burden, but as a source of power.

Tools for Managing the Ride

While the emotional rollercoaster of BPD can't be entirely avoided, it is possible to develop tools to navigate the ups and downs. These tools often involve a combination of therapy, self-awareness, and coping strategies.

1. Mindfulness: Learning to observe emotions without judgment can help reduce their intensity. Techniques like deep breathing, grounding exercises, and body scans can create a sense of calm in moments of overwhelm.

2. Emotion Regulation Skills: Dialectical Behavior Therapy (DBT) teaches practical skills for managing emotions, such as identifying triggers, reframing negative thoughts, and practicing self-soothing behaviors.

3. Self-Validation: Many women with BPD struggle with self-criticism, blaming themselves for their emotional reactions. Learning to validate your own feelings—recognizing that they are real and valid even if they feel overwhelming—can be a

transformative step.

4. Support Systems: Building a network of trusted friends, family, or therapists who understand your struggles can provide a sense of stability and reassurance.

Sarah found solace in a DBT group, where she met other women who shared her experiences. "For the first time, I didn't feel alone," she said. "I realized that my emotions didn't make me broken—they made me human."

Rewriting the Narrative

One of the most powerful ways to cope with the emotional rollercoaster of BPD is to rewrite the narrative. Instead of seeing yourself as a victim of your emotions, you can begin to see yourself as someone who feels deeply and has the capacity to grow.

For Sarah, this shift came gradually. Through therapy, she learned to recognize her triggers and develop healthier responses. Instead of spiraling into panic when her boyfriend didn't text back, she practiced grounding herself in the present moment and reminding herself of his consistent care and support. Over time, these small shifts added up, allowing her to regain a sense of control.

A New Perspective

Living with BPD means living with intensity. While this intensity can be challenging, it also brings with it a profound depth of feeling and connection. By understanding and managing emotional dysregulation, women like Sarah can learn to navigate their rollercoaster with grace and resilience.

In the next chapter, we'll explore how these emotional challenges play out in relationships—the joys, the struggles, and the path to building healthier connections.

3

Love and Relationships: Walking the Tightrope

For many women with Borderline Personality Disorder (BPD), relationships are both a source of intense joy and profound pain. The desire for connection is deeply felt, yet the fear of abandonment looms large, creating a push-pull dynamic that can leave both the individual and their partner emotionally exhausted. Navigating love, whether romantic, familial, or platonic, becomes a delicate balancing act—a tightrope walk where even small missteps feel catastrophic.

This chapter delves into the unique challenges women with BPD face in their relationships, the underlying causes of these struggles, and the tools that can help them build healthier, more fulfilling connections. Along the way, we'll hear from Priya, a 29-year-old woman whose experiences highlight both the difficulties and the possibilities of love with BPD.

The Paradox of Intimacy

At the core of BPD is an intense fear of abandonment. This fear often drives women to seek closeness with others, sometimes at the expense of their own boundaries or well-being. Yet, the very act of seeking intimacy can trigger anxiety and mistrust, leading to a cycle of idealization and devaluation.

Priya described her relationships as "all or nothing." In the early stages, she would pour herself into her partner, showering them with love and attention. "I wanted to be perfect for them, to prove I was worth staying for," she explained. But as soon as her partner failed to meet her expectations—whether by forgetting an anniversary or taking too long to reply to a text—her feelings would flip. "I'd go from loving them to feeling like they didn't care about me at all," she said. "It was like my brain couldn't hold the good and bad parts of them at the same time."

This black-and-white thinking, known as splitting, is a common feature of BPD and can make relationships feel like an emotional rollercoaster for everyone involved.

Roots of Relationship Challenges

To understand why relationships are so challenging for women with BPD, it's important to look at the underlying factors:

1. Attachment Trauma: Many individuals with BPD have histories of inconsistent or unstable caregiving during childhood. These early experiences can create insecure attachment styles, making it difficult to trust others or feel secure in relationships.

2. Fear of Abandonment: This fear is not just a fleeting worry—it's a visceral, all-consuming terror. Even small perceived signs of rejection, like a change in tone or a missed call, can trigger intense emotional reactions.

3. Hyper-Sensitivity: Women with BPD often have a heightened ability to detect subtle emotional cues. While this can make them deeply empathetic partners, it can also lead to misinterpreting neutral or ambiguous signals as negative.

4. Difficulty with Boundaries: The desire to avoid abandonment can lead to overcompensation in relationships, such as ignoring one's own needs or becoming overly dependent on a partner for validation.

The Impact on Partners and Friends

Being in a relationship with someone who has BPD can be both rewarding and challenging. Partners often describe feeling deeply loved and understood but also overwhelmed by the intensity of emotional reactions and the pressure to meet unspoken expectations.

Priya's ex-boyfriend, Tom, shared, "When things were good, they were amazing. She made me feel like the center of her world. But when things went wrong, it felt like I couldn't do anything right." Over time, the constant push-and-pull dynamic took a toll on their relationship, leaving both feeling drained and misunderstood.

Friendships can also be affected. Priya often worried that her friends secretly disliked her or would abandon her if she wasn't constantly available. This led her to overextend herself, saying yes to every invitation and ignoring her own needs, only to later resent her friends for not reciprocating.

Breaking the Cycle: Tools for Healthier Relationships

While the challenges of relationships with BPD are significant, they are not insurmountable. With self-awareness, therapy, and communication, it is possible to build connections that are both supportive and stable.

1. Understanding Triggers: Identifying the situations or behaviors that trigger feelings of abandonment or mistrust can help women with BPD respond more thoughtfully. For Priya, this meant recognizing that her fear of being ignored often stemmed from her own insecurities rather than her partner's actions.

2. Practicing Self-Validation: Relying solely on external validation can put immense pressure on relationships. Learning to validate one's own feelings and worth can create a stronger sense of self and reduce dependency on others.

3. Building Boundaries: Healthy relationships require clear boundaries. This means learning to say no, prioritizing one's own needs, and respecting the autonomy of others. Priya worked

with her therapist to set boundaries around how much time she spent with her friends and partner, ensuring she didn't lose herself in her relationships.

4. Using Communication Tools: Expressing emotions in a constructive way is key. Techniques like "I feel" statements and active listening can help avoid misunderstandings and reduce conflict. For example, instead of accusing her partner of not caring, Priya learned to say, "I feel hurt when I don't hear from you because it makes me worry about our connection."

5. Seeking Professional Support: Therapy, particularly Dialectical Behavior Therapy (DBT), can provide invaluable tools for managing relationship challenges. DBT teaches skills like interpersonal effectiveness, which helps individuals balance their needs with those of others.

When Relationships End

Despite the best efforts, some relationships will inevitably end. For women with BPD, breakups can feel devastating, often triggering feelings of abandonment, worthlessness, and despair.

When Priya's relationship with Tom ended, she initially spiraled into self-blame and hopelessness. "I felt like I'd lost the only person who could ever love me," she said. But through therapy, she began to reframe the breakup as an opportunity for growth.

"I realized that I was putting too much pressure on him to fill a void that only I could fill," she explained.

Learning to grieve a relationship without falling into destructive patterns is a vital step in the healing process.

The Possibility of Love

While relationships with BPD are challenging, they are also deeply rewarding. Women with BPD bring unique strengths to their connections, including intense empathy, passion, and the ability to love deeply. By addressing the underlying fears and patterns that drive relationship struggles, it is possible to build connections that are not only stable but also deeply fulfilling.

Priya's journey is a testament to this possibility. After years of struggle, she began dating again with a newfound sense of self-awareness and confidence. "I'm learning to love without losing myself," she said. "And that's the best kind of love there is."

A Step Forward

Relationships are one of the most complex and meaningful aspects of life. For women with BPD, they present unique challenges—but also unique opportunities for growth and connection. By embracing the tools of self-awareness, communication, and therapy, it is possible to walk the tightrope of love with grace and stability.

In the next chapter, we will explore the deeply personal struggle with identity that many women with BPD face and the journey toward discovering who they truly are.

4

The Struggle with Identity

"I don't know who I am." It's a sentiment often expressed by women with Borderline Personality Disorder (BPD), and for good reason. A shifting, unstable sense of self is one of the core features of the condition. For many, it feels like wearing a series of masks—changing roles, values, and behaviors to fit different situations or people—without a clear understanding of who they are beneath it all. This identity crisis doesn't just affect the individual; it ripples into every aspect of their lives, from relationships to careers to personal fulfillment.

In this chapter, we'll explore the origins of identity disturbances in BPD, how they manifest, and the strategies that can help women reconnect with their true selves. We'll also meet Layla, a 34-year-old woman whose journey highlights the complexities of building a stable identity.

The Roots of Identity Disturbance

To understand why identity issues are so prevalent in BPD, it's important to examine their origins. Identity is often formed in childhood through a combination of internal and external factors—personal experiences, relationships, cultural influences, and the way caregivers reflect back who we are. For individuals with BPD, this developmental process is frequently disrupted.

Layla's childhood, like that of many women with BPD, was marked by inconsistency. Her parents' volatile relationship created an environment of unpredictability, where affection and criticism were doled out unevenly. "One day I was the perfect daughter, the next I couldn't do anything right," she recalled. Over time, Layla internalized these conflicting messages, leaving her with a fractured sense of self.

Invalidation also plays a key role. When a child's emotions or perspectives are dismissed, they may struggle to trust their own experiences or instincts. Instead, they look to others for validation, adopting external values and behaviors in an effort to feel accepted.

The Chameleon Effect

One of the hallmarks of identity disturbance in BPD is a tendency to adapt to the expectations or preferences of others. This "chameleon effect" can make women with BPD highly empathetic and socially intuitive, but it also comes at a cost. Without a stable core identity, it's easy to lose oneself in relationships or social roles.

For Layla, this meant becoming whoever she thought others wanted her to be. In her twenties, she cycled through friend groups, adopting their interests and values as her own. "One year I was into yoga and clean eating because my friends were, and the next I was into partying and nightlife," she explained. "I was always looking for a group or identity that felt like home, but nothing ever did."

The Crisis of Self-Doubt

The absence of a stable identity can lead to chronic self-doubt. Women with BPD often describe feeling like imposters in their own lives, questioning their choices, achievements, and relationships. This inner turmoil can manifest as:

Career Instability: Difficulty committing to a single career path or feeling unfulfilled in professional roles.

Moral Ambiguity: Shifting values or beliefs based on external influences.

Emotional Exhaustion: The mental strain of constantly questioning one's decisions or worth.

Layla's professional life mirrored her internal struggle. Despite excelling in her job as a graphic designer, she frequently doubted her abilities and considered switching careers. "I'd get excited about something new, thinking it would finally feel right," she said. "But then the excitement would fade, and I'd feel lost all over again."

The Role of Emotional Dysregulation

Emotional dysregulation exacerbates identity disturbances, creating a feedback loop of instability. When emotions are intense and fleeting, it becomes difficult to maintain a consistent sense of self. One day, a woman with BPD might feel confident and capable; the next, she might feel like a failure. These shifts can make it hard to set long-term goals or maintain a cohesive narrative about who she is.

For Layla, this emotional volatility was particularly evident in her relationships. After a heated argument with her partner, she often questioned whether she was a good girlfriend—or even a good person. "It was like my entire self-worth hinged on how someone else saw me in that moment," she admitted.

Rebuilding the Self: Strategies for Identity Formation

While the struggle with identity is a significant challenge in BPD, it is not insurmountable. Through therapy, self-reflection, and intentional practices, women can begin to build a more stable and authentic sense of self.

1. Exploring Core Values: Identifying personal values can provide a foundation for decision-making and self-definition. Layla's therapist encouraged her to write down the qualities she admired in others and reflect on which ones resonated with her. Over time, she began to define her own values, such as creativity, kindness, and resilience.

2. Practicing Self-Compassion: Letting go of self-criticism and embracing self-compassion can help women with BPD accept themselves as they are. Techniques like journaling and affirmations can reinforce positive self-beliefs.

3. Engaging in Identity-Strengthening Activities: Trying new hobbies, volunteering, or pursuing education can help women explore their interests and talents. Layla joined a local art group, which not only reignited her passion for painting but also gave her a sense of community.

4. Grounding in the Present Moment: Mindfulness practices can help women reconnect with their inner selves, reducing the influence of external pressures. Meditation, deep breathing, or yoga are effective ways to cultivate this awareness.

5. Therapy and Support Groups: Working with a therapist or joining a support group can provide guidance and validation during the journey of self-discovery. Dialectical Behavior Therapy (DBT) is particularly effective, offering tools for emotion regulation, interpersonal effectiveness, and self-awareness.

The Journey Toward Authenticity

Rebuilding a sense of self is not a linear process. There will be setbacks and moments of doubt, but each step forward is a victory. For Layla, the journey was as much about unlearning old patterns as it was about discovering new ones. "I realized that I didn't have to be everything for everyone," she said. "I just had to be me."

Over time, Layla began to make choices that aligned with her values, rather than the expectations of others. She pursued a career in freelance graphic design, allowing her to combine her creativity with her need for flexibility. In her personal life, she set boundaries with friends and family, ensuring she had space to focus on her own needs.

A New Foundation

The struggle with identity is one of the most challenging aspects of BPD, but it is also one of the most transformative. By confronting the uncertainty and embracing the process of self-discovery, women with BPD can build a foundation that feels authentic and empowering.

5

Navigating the Healthcare System

For women with Borderline Personality Disorder (BPD), accessing effective and compassionate healthcare can feel like an uphill battle. The stigma surrounding BPD, coupled with gaps in understanding and resources within the healthcare system, often leaves women feeling misunderstood, dismissed, or even blamed for their condition. Yet, navigating this system is a critical step toward healing and recovery.

In this chapter, we will explore the challenges women with BPD face in seeking care, the systemic barriers that contribute to these struggles, and practical strategies for self-advocacy and finding the right support. Alongside these discussions, we will follow Yasmin, a 27-year-old woman whose experiences highlight both the frustrations and the triumphs of navigating the healthcare landscape.

The Stigma of BPD in Healthcare

BPD is one of the most stigmatized mental health conditions, even among healthcare professionals. Women with BPD are often labeled as "manipulative," "attention-seeking," or "difficult"—terms that not only ignore the complexity of the condition but also harm those seeking care. This stigma can lead to dismissive attitudes, misdiagnoses, and a lack of access to appropriate treatment.

Yasmin's first encounter with mental health services was after a suicide attempt in her early twenties. Instead of receiving empathy and support, she was met with judgment. "The doctor told me I just needed to 'calm down and stop overreacting,'" she recalled. "It made me feel like my pain wasn't real, like I didn't deserve help." This experience, unfortunately, is all too common for women with BPD.

Barriers to Diagnosis and Treatment

Several systemic barriers complicate the path to diagnosis and treatment for women with BPD:

1. Diagnostic Ambiguity: The symptoms of BPD often overlap with other mental health conditions, such as depression, anxiety, or bipolar disorder. This can lead to misdiagnoses and delays in receiving appropriate care.

2. Gender Bias: Women are more likely to have their emotions pathologized, leading to stereotypes that reinforce stigma. Instead of being seen as individuals in need of care, they are often dismissed as "too emotional" or "overly sensitive."

3. Lack of Specialist Services: Many mental health services are not equipped to provide the specialized care BPD requires, such as Dialectical Behavior Therapy (DBT). Long waiting lists and limited availability of trained professionals further compound this issue.

4. Financial and Geographic Barriers: Access to mental health care can depend on a person's location and financial resources, leaving many women unable to afford or reach the treatment they need.

The Importance of Advocacy

In the face of these challenges, self-advocacy becomes a crucial skill. While it is unfair that women with BPD must often fight for the care they deserve, knowing how to navigate the system can make a significant difference.

1. Educate Yourself: Understanding BPD and the treatments available can empower you to advocate for specific therapies, such as DBT. Yasmin began reading books and online resources about BPD, which gave her the confidence to request a referral to a DBT program.

2. Communicate Clearly: When speaking with healthcare providers, describe your symptoms and experiences as clearly as possible. If you feel dismissed, don't hesitate to ask for a second opinion or to escalate your concerns.

3. Know Your Rights: Familiarize yourself with patient rights in your healthcare system. In the UK, for example, individuals have

the right to request specific treatments and to file complaints if they feel they have been treated unfairly.

4. Build a Support Network: Having an advocate, such as a trusted friend, family member, or peer supporter, can help you navigate appointments and communicate your needs effectively.

Finding the Right Therapist

Therapeutic relationships are foundational to recovery for women with BPD, but finding the right therapist can be challenging. It's important to look for a professional who is experienced with BPD and who approaches the condition with empathy and understanding.

When Yasmin finally connected with a therapist trained in DBT, she noticed an immediate difference. "She didn't make me feel broken or impossible to help," Yasmin said. "She saw me as a person, not just a diagnosis." This shift in perspective allowed Yasmin to engage more fully in her treatment and begin the process of healing.

Here are some tips for finding the right therapist:

Ask Questions: During initial consultations, ask about the therapist's experience with BPD and their approach to treatment.

Trust Your Gut: A good therapeutic relationship is built on trust and rapport. If you don't feel comfortable with a therapist, it's okay to seek someone else.

Explore Alternatives: If traditional therapy isn't accessible, consider online therapy platforms, support groups, or peer-led programs.

The Role of Peer Support

Peer support can be a valuable complement to professional treatment. Connecting with others who have lived experience of BPD provides a sense of community and validation that is often missing in traditional healthcare settings.

Yasmin joined a peer support group where she met women who shared similar struggles. "For the first time, I didn't feel alone," she said. "Hearing their stories gave me hope that things could get better." Peer support groups can also be a source of practical advice, from navigating the healthcare system to coping with daily challenges.

Advocating for Systemic Change

While individual advocacy is essential, systemic change is equally important.   Women with BPD deserve access to compassionate, evidence-based care without stigma or barriers. Advocacy efforts at the community, organizational, and policy levels can help create a more inclusive and effective mental health system.

Yasmin became involved in local mental health advocacy, sharing her story to raise awareness about BPD. "I realized that speaking out wasn't just about me," she said. "It was about making things better for the next woman who walks through that door."

A Path Forward

Navigating the healthcare system as a woman with BPD is not without its challenges, but it is a journey worth taking. By educating themselves, advocating for their needs, and seeking supportive professionals and peers, women can access the care they deserve and begin the process of healing.

For Yasmin, the road to recovery was long and often difficult, but it was also transformative. "I learned that I wasn't too much or too broken," she said. "I just needed the right support to help me find my way."

Looking Ahead

Accessing care is only the first step in the journey of managing BPD. In the next chapter, we will explore Dialectical Behavior Therapy (DBT) in depth—its core components, how it addresses the challenges of BPD, and the transformative potential it offers for women seeking to reclaim their lives.

6

Breaking the Cycle with Dialectical Behavior Therapy (DBT)

For women with Borderline Personality Disorder (BPD), navigating life can feel like constantly treading water in a stormy sea. Emotions rise and crash unpredictably, leaving them overwhelmed and exhausted. Dialectical Behavior Therapy (DBT) offers a life raft—practical tools and strategies that not only help women stay afloat but also teach them to navigate the waves with greater confidence and control.

In this chapter, we will explore the origins and core components of DBT, how it addresses the unique challenges of BPD, and real-world examples of its transformative effects. We'll also follow Maya, a 30-year-old woman who used DBT to reclaim her life after years of chaos and pain.

What is Dialectical Behavior Therapy?

DBT was developed in the 1980s by Dr. Marsha Linehan, a psychologist who recognized the limitations of traditional cognitive-behavioral therapy (CBT) for individuals with intense emotional dysregulation. Combining elements of CBT with mindfulness and acceptance strategies, DBT was specifically designed to address the challenges of BPD.

The term "dialectical" reflects the central principle of the therapy: balancing acceptance and change. For women with BPD, this means learning to accept their emotions and experiences while simultaneously working to change the behaviors and thought patterns that cause distress.

The Four Core Components of DBT

DBT is structured around four key skill modules, each targeting a specific area of difficulty:

1. Mindfulness

Mindfulness is the foundation of DBT, teaching women to stay present and observe their thoughts and emotions without judgment. For Maya, mindfulness became a tool to pause and reflect rather than react impulsively. "It helped me realize that my emotions weren't facts," she explained. "Just because I felt abandoned didn't mean I actually was."

2. Distress Tolerance

Distress tolerance focuses on building resilience in the face of emotional crises. Skills like grounding exercises, distraction techniques, and self-soothing help women ride out intense emotions without resorting to harmful behaviors. Maya found comfort in holding an ice cube during moments of overwhelming anger or sadness, using the cold sensation to anchor herself in the present.

3. Emotional Regulation

Emotional regulation skills help women understand and manage their emotions more effectively. By identifying triggers and practicing techniques like opposite action—choosing behaviors that counteract negative emotions—Maya learned to de-escalate her emotional responses. For example, when she felt rejected, instead of isolating herself, she would reach out to a friend for support.

4. Interpersonal Effectiveness

Interpersonal effectiveness skills focus on improving relationships by teaching women how to assert their needs, set boundaries, and handle conflict constructively. Maya used these skills to rebuild her relationship with her mother, learning to express her feelings without blame or hostility. "For the first time, I felt like we were really listening to each other," she said.

The Structure of DBT

DBT is typically delivered in a combination of individual therapy and group skills training:

Individual Therapy: Provides a space to address personal challenges, develop coping strategies, and apply DBT skills to real-life situations.

Group Skills Training: Offers a supportive environment to learn and practice DBT skills alongside others with similar struggles.

Maya initially felt hesitant about joining a group, fearing judgment from others. However, she quickly found it to be one of the most valuable aspects of DBT. "Hearing other people's stories made me feel less alone," she said. "We were all learning and growing together."

Transforming BPD Through DBT

DBT's effectiveness for BPD is well-documented, with studies showing significant reductions in self-harm, suicidal ideation, emotional instability, and interpersonal conflict. What makes DBT particularly powerful is its holistic approach—it doesn't just address symptoms but also equips women with the tools to build meaningful, fulfilling lives.

For Maya, this transformation was gradual but profound. Over the course of a year in DBT, she noticed significant changes in how she handled challenges. Arguments with her partner no longer spiraled into threats of leaving or self-harm. Instead, she used her interpersonal effectiveness skills to communicate her feelings and needs. At work, she felt more confident setting boundaries with her colleagues, reducing the burnout that had plagued her for years.

Overcoming Challenges in DBT

While DBT is highly effective, it's not without its challenges. Learning new skills and breaking old patterns requires time, effort, and commitment. Many women struggle with the initial discomfort of confronting their emotions and changing ingrained behaviors.

Maya faced these challenges head-on. "There were times when I wanted to quit," she admitted. "But my therapist reminded me that progress isn't about perfection—it's about persistence." Her perseverance paid off, as each small step forward built momentum for larger changes.

Integrating DBT Into Daily Life

One of DBT's greatest strengths is its practicality. The skills taught in DBT can be integrated into daily life, providing a toolkit for navigating everything from minor frustrations to major crises. Maya kept a DBT diary card—a tool used to track emotions, behaviors, and skill use—which helped her stay accountable and recognize her progress over time.

Some of the strategies she found most helpful included:

The STOP Skill: Stop, Take a step back, Observe, Proceed mindfully. This technique helped Maya pause before reacting impulsively in emotionally charged situations.

Radical Acceptance: Embracing reality as it is, rather than fighting against it, allowed Maya to let go of resentment and focus on what she could control.

DEAR MAN Framework: Describe, Express, Assert, Reinforce, Mindful, Appear confident, Negotiate. This interpersonal effectiveness tool helped Maya communicate her needs clearly and respectfully.

The Long-Term Benefits of DBT

DBT is not a quick fix, but its impact can be life-changing. For women with BPD, the skills learned in DBT provide a foundation for continued growth and resilience. Maya described it as "a guidebook for living" that she could return to whenever she faced challenges.

"I still have hard days," she said. "But now I have the tools to get through them. DBT gave me my life back—it gave me hope."

A New Chapter

Breaking the cycle of BPD is not an easy journey, but it is a journey worth taking. For women like Maya, DBT offers more than just symptom relief—it offers a path to self-discovery, empowerment, and lasting change.

In the next chapter, we will explore how women with BPD navigate the workplace, balancing ambition with mental health and creating environments where they can thrive.

7

Thriving in the Workplace

The workplace is a complex arena for women with Borderline Personality Disorder (BPD). It can be a source of empowerment, structure, and purpose, but it can also amplify stressors like interpersonal conflict, self-doubt, and emotional exhaustion. Many women with BPD struggle to find stability in their careers, often feeling misunderstood or unsupported in environments that demand emotional control and resilience.

In this chapter, we will explore the unique challenges women with BPD face in professional settings, strategies for navigating these difficulties, and the steps employers can take to create more inclusive workplaces. Alongside this discussion, we'll follow Rachel, a 33-year-old marketing manager whose journey highlights both the struggles and triumphs of balancing BPD and career success.

The Challenges of BPD in the Workplace

Women with BPD often describe the workplace as a microcosm of the emotional and relational challenges they face in their personal lives. The high stakes of professional environments— where reputations, promotions, and livelihoods are on the line— can magnify the intensity of BPD symptoms.

Emotional Volatility

Rachel often felt that her emotions were "too big" for the office. A minor critique from her supervisor could spiral into hours of self-doubt, while a disagreement with a colleague could leave her feeling rejected and unvalued. "I always felt like I was on edge," she explained. "One bad interaction could ruin my entire day."

Imposter Syndrome

The unstable sense of self that accompanies BPD can make it difficult to feel confident in professional roles. Rachel frequently questioned whether she deserved her accomplishments, attributing her successes to luck rather than skill. "No matter how hard I worked, I never felt like I belonged," she said.

Interpersonal Challenges

The push-pull dynamic common in relationships for women with BPD often extends to colleagues and supervisors. Rachel found herself idealizing certain colleagues, only to later resent them for perceived slights. "It felt like I was constantly walking a tightrope in my relationships at work," she said.

Strategies for Thriving at Work

Despite these challenges, women with BPD can build fulfilling careers by developing strategies to manage their symptoms and create supportive environments.

1. Prioritize Self-Awareness

Understanding how BPD affects your behavior and emotions in the workplace is the first step toward making positive changes. Rachel worked with her therapist to identify her triggers at work, such as tight deadlines and ambiguous feedback. "Once I knew what set me off, I could start planning ways to handle those situations," she explained.

2. Develop Coping Mechanisms

Practical coping strategies can help women with BPD navigate stressful situations at work:

Use Mindfulness Techniques: Grounding exercises, such as focusing on your breath or observing your surroundings, can help you stay present during moments of overwhelm.

Take Breaks: Stepping away from your desk for a few minutes can help reset your emotions and prevent escalation.

Set Realistic Goals: Breaking tasks into smaller, manageable steps can reduce the sense of being overwhelmed.

3. Communicate Effectively

Clear communication is essential in the workplace, particularly for women with BPD who may struggle with assumptions or misinterpretations. Rachel used DBT's DEAR MAN framework to advocate for herself during a performance review. "I explained my needs without getting defensive, and it completely changed the conversation," she said.

4. Build a Support System

Having trusted colleagues or mentors who understand your challenges can make a significant difference. Rachel confided in a supportive coworker, who became an ally and advocate for her in team meetings. "Knowing I had someone in my corner helped me feel less alone," she said.

5. Set Boundaries

Maintaining healthy boundaries is critical for avoiding burnout and protecting your emotional well-being. Rachel learned to say no to additional responsibilities when she was already stretched thin, even though it initially felt uncomfortable. "I realized that setting limits wasn't selfish—it was necessary," she said.

When and How to Disclose BPD at Work

Deciding whether to disclose a BPD diagnosis at work is a deeply personal decision that depends on factors such as workplace culture, relationships with supervisors, and the individual's comfort level. While disclosure can lead to accommodations and understanding, it also carries risks, particularly in environments where mental health stigma persists.

Considerations Before Disclosing

Assess the Culture: Does your workplace have a supportive approach to mental health? Are there clear policies for accommodations?

Identify the Purpose: What do you hope to gain by disclosing? Are you seeking specific accommodations or simply aiming to build understanding?

Choose the Right Person: Disclose to someone you trust, such as a supervisor, HR representative, or mentor.

How Rachel Navigated Disclosure

After struggling with emotional exhaustion, Rachel decided to disclose her BPD diagnosis to her manager. "I framed it in terms of what I needed to succeed," she said. "I asked for regular check-ins and clearer deadlines, which made a huge difference in my performance and stress levels."

What Employers Can Do

Employers play a critical role in creating workplaces where women with BPD can thrive. By fostering a culture of inclusivity and support, organizations can empower all employees to reach their full potential.

1. Educate Staff

Training on mental health awareness and stigma reduction can help employees and managers better understand conditions like BPD. This education can create a more empathetic and supportive workplace culture.

2. Provide Accommodations

Reasonable accommodations, such as flexible scheduling, regular feedback, or access to quiet spaces, can help women with BPD manage their symptoms without compromising their productivity.

3. Encourage Open Dialogue

Promoting a culture where mental health is openly discussed and supported can reduce the fear of disclosure and create a sense of belonging for employees with BPD.

Redefining Success

For Rachel, learning to thrive at work was about more than managing symptoms—it was about redefining success on her own terms. By embracing her unique strengths, such as creativity and empathy, she found a sense of purpose and fulfillment in her career. "I stopped trying to fit into a mold that wasn't made for me," she said. "I started building a career that felt authentic to who I am."

A New Perspective

The workplace can be a challenging environment for women with BPD, but it can also be a space for growth, connection, and achievement. With self-awareness, coping strategies, and support from colleagues and employers, women can not only survive but thrive in their careers.

In the next chapter, we will explore the power of connection, focusing on the importance of building and maintaining supportive relationships in the journey toward healing and resilience.

8

Healing Through Connection

Human beings are wired for connection. For women with Borderline Personality Disorder (BPD), however, relationships can feel like both a lifeline and a battlefield. The desire for deep, meaningful bonds is often accompanied by fear, mistrust, and a history of relational pain. Yet, building and maintaining healthy connections is not only possible but also essential for healing and growth.

In this chapter, we'll explore the transformative power of connection, the challenges of forming and sustaining relationships, and practical strategies for nurturing healthy bonds. We'll also follow Sofia, a 38-year-old woman whose journey from isolation to connection highlights the resilience and courage required to open up to others.

The Dual Nature of Connection in BPD

For women with BPD, relationships are often marked by a push-pull dynamic. The deep longing for connection can be overshadowed by fears of abandonment or rejection, leading to patterns of idealization and devaluation. This duality creates intense, and often tumultuous, relational experiences.

Sofia described her relationships as "all or nothing." In her twenties, she poured herself into friendships, often prioritizing others' needs over her own. But the smallest perceived slight—a canceled plan or a forgotten text—could trigger feelings of betrayal and lead her to cut ties. "I wanted to be close to people, but it always felt like I was getting hurt," she said.

The Challenges of Building Connections

Fear of Abandonment

The fear of being abandoned or left behind is a central struggle for women with BPD. This fear can lead to behaviors like clinging to relationships, avoiding conflict, or testing others' loyalty, which may unintentionally strain bonds.

Trust Issues

Past experiences of rejection, betrayal, or invalidation can make it difficult to trust others. Women with BPD may second-guess others' intentions or withdraw out of self-protection, even in relationships that are fundamentally safe.

Emotional Intensity

The heightened emotions characteristic of BPD can make relationships feel overwhelming. Expressing feelings in ways that others perceive as "too much" can lead to misunderstandings or alienation.

Difficulty with Boundaries

The desire for closeness can blur the lines between healthy and unhealthy behaviors. Women with BPD may struggle to assert their needs or respect others' boundaries, creating tension in relationships.

The Healing Power of Connection

Despite these challenges, relationships have the potential to be a powerful source of healing for women with BPD. Supportive connections provide validation, stability, and a sense of belonging that can counteract the isolation and self-doubt often experienced with the condition.

Sofia found this healing power in her relationship with her sister, Elena. "She never gave up on me, even when I pushed her away," Sofia said. "Her patience and love helped me believe that I was worth fighting for."

Strategies for Building Healthy Connections

1. Start with Yourself Healing through connection begins with developing a healthier relationship with yourself. Self-compassion, self-care, and self-awareness create a foundation for authentic relationships with others. Sofia's therapist encouraged her to journal about her strengths and

achievements, helping her build self-esteem and reduce reliance on external validation.

2. Communicate Openly Clear, honest communication is essential for building trust and understanding. Using "I feel" statements and expressing needs without blame can help prevent misunderstandings. Sofia practiced saying, "I feel hurt when plans change because it makes me worry about being forgotten," instead of accusing her friends of not caring.

3. Set and Respect Boundaries Healthy boundaries are vital for maintaining balanced relationships. This includes recognizing your limits, asserting your needs, and respecting the boundaries of others. Sofia learned to say no to social events when she felt overwhelmed, ensuring she had the energy to show up fully for her closest relationships.

4. Practice Mindfulness in Relationships Mindfulness can help women with BPD stay present in their interactions, reducing the influence of past traumas or future anxieties. Techniques like deep breathing or focusing on the sensations of the moment can create space for thoughtful responses rather than impulsive reactions.

5. Seek Out Supportive Communities Connecting with people who share similar experiences can provide a sense of belonging and validation. Sofia joined a peer support group for women

with BPD, where she found understanding and encouragement. "It was the first time I didn't feel like I had to explain myself," she said.

Rebuilding Relationships After Conflict

Conflict is a natural part of any relationship, but for women with BPD, it can feel catastrophic. The intense emotions that arise during disagreements can lead to impulsive actions or words that damage relationships. However, repair is always possible with genuine effort and accountability.

Steps to Rebuild Trust

1. Acknowledge Your Role: Take responsibility for your actions without self-blame or defensiveness.

2. Apologize Sincerely: Express genuine regret for the harm caused and commit to doing better.

3. Listen Actively: Allow the other person to share their feelings and perspectives without interruption or judgment.

4. Show Consistency: Demonstrate your commitment to change through consistent actions over time.

When Sofia had an argument with Elena, she initially withdrew, fearing rejection. But with the encouragement of her therapist, she reached out to apologize. "I told her I was sorry for shutting her out and explained why I reacted the way I did," Sofia said. "It wasn't easy, but it brought us closer."

The Role of Professional Support

Therapists and support groups can play a crucial role in helping women with BPD navigate relationships. Therapists can provide guidance on effective communication, emotional regulation, and boundary-setting, while support groups offer a safe space to share experiences and gain insight from others.

Sofia's DBT group included a module on interpersonal effectiveness, which she found invaluable. "It taught me how to express my needs without fear," she said. "I started using those skills in all my relationships, and it made a huge difference."

A Network of Resilience

Healing through connection is not about creating perfect relationships—it's about building a network of resilience that supports growth, understanding, and mutual care. For Sofia, this meant embracing the imperfections of both herself and others. "I realized that no relationship is perfect," she said. "What matters is showing up for each other and working through the tough moments together."

A Bridge to the Future

Connection is both a challenge and a gift for women with BPD. While the path to healthy relationships requires effort and vulnerability, the rewards—trust, support, and belonging—are immeasurable. By fostering meaningful connections, women can create a bridge to healing, resilience, and a more fulfilling life.

In the next and final chapter, we will explore what it means to move beyond survival and embrace a life of purpose, self-discovery, and fulfillment.

9

Beyond Survival: Living a Fulfilling Life

For women with Borderline Personality Disorder (BPD), the journey of healing often begins with survival—managing intense emotions, building healthier relationships, and finding stability. But recovery is about more than just surviving; it's about thriving. It's about moving beyond the label of BPD, reclaiming your identity, and building a life filled with purpose, joy, and meaning.

In this final chapter, we'll explore what it means to live a fulfilling life with BPD, the tools for sustaining growth, and stories of resilience that prove recovery is not only possible but also transformative. We'll also revisit the stories of the women we've met throughout this book to see how they've embraced their futures.

Reframing BPD: From Burden to Strength

The first step to thriving is redefining how you see yourself and your diagnosis. BPD doesn't have to be a burden; it can be a source of strength. The same emotional intensity that feels overwhelming can also fuel empathy, creativity, and passion. By embracing these traits, women with BPD can find meaning and purpose in their lives.

Sofia, who struggled with self-doubt and relationship challenges, began to see her sensitivity as a gift. "I realized that my ability to feel deeply wasn't a weakness—it was a strength," she said. "It allowed me to connect with others in a way that felt real and authentic."

Pursuing Passion and Purpose

A fulfilling life often includes pursuing passions and finding purpose, whether through career, art, activism, or personal growth. For many women with BPD, discovering what brings them joy can be a journey of trial and error—but it's one worth taking.

1. Rediscovering Hobbies and Interests

Hobbies provide a sense of accomplishment and an outlet for self-expression. Rachel, who found stability at work, reignited her love for photography, capturing moments of beauty and connection in her daily life. "Photography became my way of seeing the world differently," she said. "It helped me focus on the present and appreciate the little things."

2. Giving Back

Volunteering or mentoring others can create a sense of purpose and belonging. Anya, who overcame self-harm, now shares her story in mental health workshops, offering hope to others. "Helping others gave my struggles meaning," she said. "It reminded me that I wasn't alone."

3. Setting Goals

Setting realistic, meaningful goals can provide direction and motivation. Layla, who once felt lost in her identity, set a goal to complete a yoga teacher training program. "It gave me something to work toward," she said. "Each step felt like a small victory."

Sustaining Growth

Thriving with BPD is an ongoing process that requires effort, self-awareness, and a commitment to growth. Here are some tools for sustaining progress:

1. Continuing Therapy

Therapy remains a valuable resource for managing challenges and exploring new opportunities. Whether through DBT, individual counseling, or group support, staying connected to therapeutic resources can provide stability and guidance.

2. Practicing Self-Care

Self-care is essential for maintaining emotional well-being.

This includes not only physical care, such as exercise and nutrition, but also emotional care, such as journaling, mindfulness, or spending time with loved ones.

3. Building a Support Network

Surrounding yourself with supportive, understanding people can help you navigate life's challenges. Yasmin, who once struggled with healthcare stigma, found strength in her peer support group. "They became my anchor," she said. "We celebrated each other's wins and lifted each other up during tough times."

4. Embracing Flexibility

Recovery is not linear, and setbacks are a natural part of the process. Learning to adapt and approach challenges with curiosity rather than self-criticism can make setbacks less daunting.

Stories of Resilience

Throughout this book, we've followed the journeys of women who faced immense challenges but chose to keep moving forward. Their stories are a testament to the resilience and strength of women with BPD:

Maya: After completing a year of DBT, Maya found stability and joy in her daily life. "DBT didn't just teach me skills—it gave me hope," she said. "I learned that I am capable of change."

Rachel: By setting boundaries and building confidence, Rachel excelled in her career and rekindled her passion for photography. "I stopped trying to be perfect and started focusing on what made me happy," she said.

Anya: Overcoming self-harm, Anya found purpose in advocacy and education, inspiring others to seek help and believe in recovery. "My pain became my power," she said.

Sofia: By nurturing her relationships and embracing her sensitivity, Sofia built a life filled with connection and love. "Healing didn't mean changing who I was—it meant accepting who I was all along," she said.

Embracing the Future

Living a fulfilling life with BPD doesn't mean the challenges disappear—it means developing the tools, relationships, and mindset to navigate those challenges with resilience and grace. It's about recognizing that your story isn't defined by your diagnosis but by the choices you make and the life you build.

For women like Sofia, Rachel, Anya, Maya, and Yasmin, the future is no longer a source of fear but a canvas for possibility. Their journeys remind us that recovery is not about erasing pain but transforming it into something meaningful.

A Final Message of Hope

To every woman reading this book, know that you are not alone. The path of healing is not easy, but it is possible. With support, self-compassion, and perseverance, you can move beyond survival and create a life that reflects your unique strengths, values, and dreams.

Your story is still unfolding, and the best chapters are yet to come.

10

Conclusion: A Journey Worth Taking

Borderline Personality Disorder is a condition that challenges every aspect of life—but it does not define who you are. Throughout this book, we've explored the complexities of BPD from the lens of women who have faced its struggles and emerged stronger. Their stories are not just tales of survival but of resilience, transformation, and hope.

Healing is a journey, not a destination. There will be moments of doubt and difficulty, but there will also be triumphs—small victories that remind you of your strength and the possibilities ahead. You have the power to reclaim your life, rewrite your story, and create a future that reflects who you truly are.

You are not alone in this journey. There is a community of women, therapists, advocates, and loved ones who believe in your ability to thrive. Lean into these connections, trust in your capacity for growth, and remember: the life you want is within reach.

Acknowledgments

This book would not have been possible without the incredible courage and honesty of the women who shared their stories. Thank you to Maya, Rachel, Sofia, Yasmin, Layla, and Anya for letting us into your lives and allowing your journeys to inspire others. Your resilience is a testament to the strength of the human spirit.

To the mental health professionals who have dedicated their careers to understanding and treating BPD, your work provides hope to countless individuals. A special acknowledgment to Dr. Marsha Linehan, whose groundbreaking work in Dialectical Behavior Therapy has transformed lives worldwide.

Finally, thank you to every reader who picked up this book. Whether you live with BPD, love someone who does, or are simply seeking to understand, your willingness to engage with these stories is a step toward greater empathy and connection.

Resources for Further Support

Books and Workbooks

The Dialectical Behavior Therapy Skills Workbook by Matthew McKay, Jeffrey C. Wood, and Jeffrey Brantley

Loving Someone with Borderline Personality Disorder by Shari Y. Manning

Coping with BPD: DBT and CBT Skills to Soothe the Symptoms

of Borderline Personality Disorder by Blaise Aguirre and Gillian Galen

Support Organizations

National Alliance on Mental Illness (NAMI): www.nami.org

Borderline Personality Disorder Resource Center (BPD Resource Center): www.borderlinepersonalitydisorder.com

Mind (UK): www.mind.org.uk

Online Communities

SANE Forums (Australia): www.sane.org

The Mighty (Mental Health): www.themighty.com

Therapy Locators

Psychology Today's Therapist Directory: www.psychologytoda y.com

Good Therapy: www.goodtherapy.org

A Final Note

Your journey is unique, but it is also shared. The women featured in this book have shown that BPD, while challenging, is not insurmountable. With the right tools, support, and mindset, you can build a life of stability, purpose, and joy. Take one step at a time, be patient with yourself, and never lose sight of the strength within you.

This is not the end—it is the beginning of your next chapter.